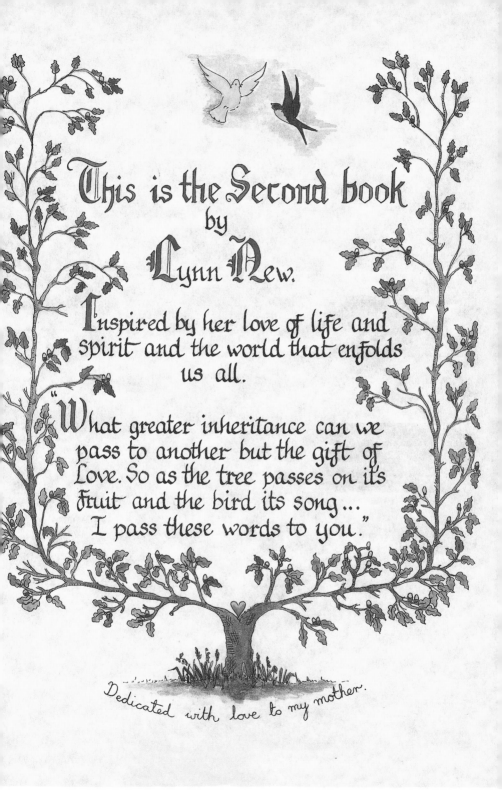

This is the Second book
by
Lynn New.

Inspired by her love of life and
spirit and the world that enfolds
us all.

"What greater inheritance can we
pass to another but the gift of
Love. So as the tree passes on it's
fruit and the bird its song...
I pass these words to you."

Dedicated with love to my mother.

Vision

How hard is the journey, how high is the climb
Yet I hold on to vision I know to be mine.
But why did I choose a pathway so steep,
A life born of longing and loving so deep?
Why did I not choose the careless of ways
And flippantly spend long, lazy days?
Why must I prove my right to exist,
To make each day worthy, not to be missed?
I climb till the day is shadowed by night;
Climb by the stars that offer their light.
Sometimes I stumble and almost am thrown
But it's then that I learn I'm not on my own.
I feel the firmness of wind on my back,
And know that perhaps it's courage I lack.
Why do I climb, though the peak I can't see,
It's because in my vision it's where I must be.

LYNN NEW ©

Seasons

"Let me sing", said the songbird,
"Let me fill my lungs with God's air,
Let me give praise to the Springtime
Let me chase away winters care."

"Let me dance", said the summer flower,
"Let me reach my bright buds to the sun,
Let me sway in the breeze through the long grass,
Give praise that the summers begun."

"Let me ripen", said the corn that is golden,
"Let me grow straight and strong in my field,
Let me bless the richness of Autumn,
Give plenty, my harvest to yield."

"Let us sleep now", said dormouse & hedgehog,
"While winter winds blow their cold chill,
Let us keep warm in God's keeping
Till spring blossoms again at His will."

LYNN NEW ©

Finding the Balance.

Where falls the sun but by a shadow?
What gift is day without a night?
Wherefore lies the meaning of
Peace without the fight?

What use are tidal pools of plenty,
Without the flood to follow through?
What meaning has the Spring abundant
Without last winter's icy hue?

What good is all the joy and gladness
If that is all you'll ever know?
Likewise those poor souls of sorrow
Who'll never feel loves little glow?

There can't be one without the other.
Can't be darkness without light.
The law of life must have its balance
Those who are blind shall treasure sight.

The lesson there, that is for learning
Lies hidden, harsh, but must be taught.
For nature holds the scales of learning
From all experience we've sought.

So when we walk our chosen pathway
Yet touch the curb of left and right,
We'll learn, in time, to walk the middle
Where balance merges dark and light.

Wishing You Well.

Sorry you are poorly
And feeling pretty low,
But when you reach the bottom
There's just one way to go.
For soon you will be better
And days won't be so long,
Then before you know it
You'll be quite well and strong;
And though you are off colour
Your health has let you down,
I send this simple message
To banish every frown.
So look upon tomorrow
As the day that you will find
Such a great improvement
And a quiet peace of mind.

LYNN NEW ©

The Farewell

Please let me go, I'm growing
And I have wings to spread,
It's true, there is a saying.
That, you're a long time dead."

I've many years before me,
As far as I can tell.
I want to live them fully,
I want to live them well.

You've always been beside me
In body or in mind,
But now it's time for flying
Knowing not what I may find.

Don't wish me back, I'm going,
For I have things to do.
I know you love me dearly
Just as I love you.

So let me go quite gladly,
Hold back the tears uncried
And let the gift of parting
Be your door kept open wide.

LYNN NEW ©

Our Grand-daughter.

Through the years we've watched you grow
and so
We thought it time we told you
How much you mean to us, no fuss,
We really want to show you,
How through your caring days and ways
We grew to love you gladly.
How when you laugh and grin, you win
Our hearts, they beat quite madly.
How quickly years do race, such chase,
So fast it seems you're growing;
How through your ups and downs
and frowns
Your 'joy of life's' still showing.
Grand parents are not always there –
that's fair.
To watch you day by day;
But you will always be beside, inside
Our hearts, and there you'll stay.

LYNN NEW ©

The Key.

What good is a door to the soul
If no one gives you the key,
No one to point you the way,
No one to help you to see?
How can we turn to the light
If in a dark room we stand?
How can we find our way out
If there is no one to hold out their hand?
Why must we first lose our way
Before we stand still and reclaim
All that in darkness we lost
If there's no one to call out our name?

All these fair questions are asked
By the many who stand behind doors,
Waiting for someone to knock,
Someone to give their lives cause.
But first my friends you must listen
Intently, and make your eyes see
That only when you ask the questions
Will you understand what is to be:
For the "Keeper of Light" will step forward
And your darkness and loss be no more,
He will hand you the key if you ask it,
But it's you who must unlock the door!

LYNN NEW ©

Missing You.

Where are you now, my friend ~ I miss you?
What pathway do you walk ~ what hills to climb?
    I have so many questions
    Unanswered at this time.

What worries do you have ~ to share or not?
What life to live ~ or walk alone?
    So many are my questions,
    But you are not at home.

What fate has lain in wait ~ horizons blue?
Who have you met ~ what do you share?
    I seek so many answers
    From my friend who isn't there.

You promised you'd return ~ or did you?
There's been no message, word or call.
    Now I'll have to question
    "Will you come back at all?"

Wherever you are now, my friend ~ I bless you:
The answer to my questions have to be ~
    The eagle of your spirit flies
    And the wolf who runs is free!"

In God's Presence.

The God in me is special
It is He who holds my hand
And makes me stand and listen
When I can't understand
What it is about me
And the world in which I live
That makes it sometimes difficult
To learn to take and give:
For the God who is so special
Knows me more than most,
He sits through twilight hours;
In my home He plays the host.
So I am never lonely
For we have much to share.
I know each day's a blessing,
For He is always there.

Thankyou

Thankyou's such a little word,
Often thought, but seldom heard.
It doesn't take that long to say
Yet on our lips it fades away.
A gentle word, a casual hand,
A caring thought, to understand.
A droplet in this cold world's pond
That sends its ripples far beyond.
For who's to know the joy it brings,
The comfort from another's wings,
Unless the word that lies so small
Becomes the greatest of them all.
Unless we learn to take and give
Appreciating who we're with:
It doesn't take too long to say
But thankyou goes a long, long way!
… Thankyou.

Affirmation

No journey shall be too long
    For You are with me,
  No hill too high, nor night too long.
I shall not look behind
    For You are in front;
I shall not be sad,
     For You shall bring my joy.
I shall not be weak when in pain
    For You are my healer
Nor dull, for You are my inspiration.
I shall be of firm hand and foot,
   Fair heart, fair smile and calm.
I shall be of one voice against all storms.
One strength against loose tongues
    and foul mouths.
I shall be all these things and more
For the One who knows me and loves me best
   Walks the pathway with my soul.

LYNN NEW ©

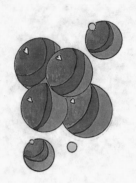

My Loving Husband.

Do not count the milestones
Of the years you've spent on earth
But count how much I love you
And truly know your worth.

It's you I really treasure
And can count the ways
How you turn my quiet hours
Into contented days.

You are my friend and lover,
My husband good and true,
And sometimes like a brother
When there's hardship to come through.

You're very special to me;
But more than that my dear,
I count my many blessings
That by my side you're near.

LYNN NEW ©

Lover's Pledge.

Sweet love, may I caress you,
And touch your lips to bless you.
My smile to warm your silent heart,
My whispered words which now impart
The love I feel at every glance
That makes my heart lift and dance.
The knowing that I now belong
Within the world of poet's song.
It's all because I recognize
The warmth of love behind your eyes.
It is in love I worship you;
Not what you say, or think, or do.
It is because of who you are,
My friend, my lover; guiding star.
Our hearts and hopes and hands entwine
When I'm with you all heaven's mine.

LYNN NEW ©

Dear Sister.

The love I truly feel for you
Too rarely have I shown,
Yet always has it been there
As side by side we've grown.

Ofcourse we've had our ups and downs,
Our laughter and our tears,
But you've been my life-long comfort
And swept away my fears.

To you I've said just what I've felt,
And from my mouth I blurt;
I know that I can be like that,
Though it may sometimes hurt.

Yet sister, should you need my help,
And loudly call my name,
You always will remember me
As the one who came!

LYNN NEW ©

Night Visitor.

He came and sat with me that night,
He kissed my troubled brow,
I told my worries to the Lord...
I know not of them now.

Through shadows falling over light,
Through the unlocked door,
He came & stood beside my bed,
My troubles are no more.

Did I see Him?
Did I look?
Did I feel His hand?
I saw Him with the eyes of love,
Can you understand?

Softly as a whispered breeze,
And silently as air
He held His hand outstretched to me
And lifted from me care.

"Arise and walk with me again
Oh child of My soul,
Be not afraid of things to come
Your knowledge shall be whole."

Did I hear Him?
Did He call?
Or whisper in my ear?
He spoke to me with voice of love,
Can you hear?

LYNN NEW ©

The Birthday Clock.

Count not your years on earth
By the setting sun,
Nor by the clock, as the hours run.
Count them by the joy, to many you have brought;
By the quality of life, which you have sought.

Count not your birthdays
By life's ageing lines,
Nor the slowing pace and tell tale signs.
Count them by the friends and company you share,
By the love that comes to you from folk who care.

Count the special memories,
Some large, some small.
Some which at the time, seemed to matter not at all.
Count the 'Birthday Wishes' which come flooding
                                          in to you;
May peace and health be with you
May future dreams come true.

LYNN NEW ©

His Gifts.

He gave me eyes to look upon Him,
And hands to touch His robe,
And feet to walk towards Him,
When lifting up lifes heavy load.

He gave me ears to hear His calling
And lips to speak His word.
He gave me arms to stop me falling
When words of comfort I'd not heard.

He gave me breath, to know what life is.
A sense of smell, so I'd rejoice,
And tears to cry, to know what strife is.
A sense of will, a gift of choice.

He gave me all life has to cherish,
A chance to fall, or start again,
To lift my heart back on His pathway,
His song of life, a sweet refrain.

The greatest gift to me He's given,
The gift of Love, how great thou art.
While on lifes journey I've been driven,
He beats within me, He is my heart.

LYNN NEW ©

The Christening

Now we see you Christened,
Gathered in His arms,
Holding you securely
Safe from all life's harms.
　　Just as the Blessing made
　　The promise shall be given
　　That you will walk your path of life
　　With the One who's truly risen.

　　For you dear little baby
　　He will safely keep,
　　Angels watching over you
　　Gently as you sleep
And through the daylight hours
Guide you on your way
Teaching you the right from wrong,
Watching as you pray.

Giving you encouragement
When you do not think He's there;
Laughing while you play,
Drying tears of your despair.
　　His Love shall know no borders
　　And He will always be
　　Standing close beside you
　　Walking steadfastly.

　　Round the font we've gathered
　　And will soon depart;
　　Blessings God has given you
　　Remain within your heart.
This time, dear child, is hallowed,
The Love of God is true,
And just as you've been brought to Him,
It's He who's come to you.

LYNN NEW ©

Tapestry of Life

And I shall weave the canvas of your life
And let you choose the silks.
Choose your colours well, to match the gifts
                                    I've chosen.
Pick them well, to suit the cloth that I
                        have woven.
Choose the brighter colours, to lift the natural grey,
To heighten and to lift the spirit on the dullest day.
Choose them for the softness of their touch,
                        and in doing such
Let them be in harmony; as the life you lead.
Choose them to be strong, not tough or harsh
                    like flax or tweed.
Work them with love, all blending,
Gently and caressing-they will need no mending:
No regrets of colours chosen;
Nor the tapestry I've woven.

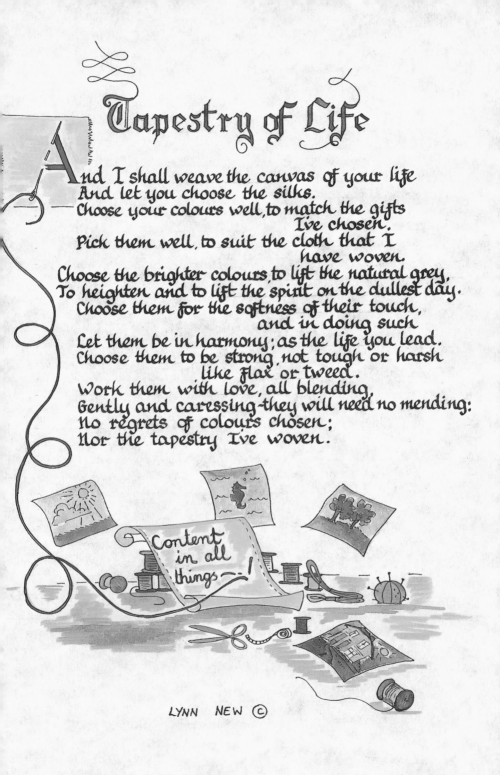

Content
in all
things ~!

Dolphin Dream.

Dolphin Friend I hear you
Gently though my sleep,
Calling me to swim beside
You, through the ocean deep.

Why do I seem to know you,
And you to know me too,
It seems that I am destined
To swim in sleep with you.

Although we are dissimilar,
Most things we can't compare,
And yet we seem to recognize
The spirit that we share.

Let me ride the waves with you,
Let me hold on tight;
Help me turn my ocean
Into a sea of light.

Although my body's weary,
In sleep my spirit's free,
And I will dream forever
Of the night I swam with thee.

Brother Mine

Brothers are so special,
Well you are, this is so;
But why is it so hard to say
And difficult to show?
I often want to tell you
How much you mean to me
But then I feel so awkward
I have to let it be.
In growing up as children
We learn to play our parts
And then we find it harder
To say what's in our hearts.
I think perhaps I'll give you
This little verse instead,
To tell you just a few things
Running through my head.
Please don't feel embarrassed,
The words you read are true;
They're not said very often
But brother – I love you.

LYNN NEW ©

The Gift of Friendship

When you give a present
No matter what it is;
Whether it says "Hers,"
Or whether it reads "His".
No matter what the cost involves,
No matter what the price —
Or "Do they really want it,
And should I take advice?"
It doesn't really matter
Though the problem can be great
You're scared you'll buy a present
That they truly hate.
Do you know, the real gift
Is not within the wrapping,
Not tied up with golden string
Or in silver trapping?
It could be just a pebble
Or shells picked from the sand,
Or the giving of encouragement;
The holding of a hand.
The gift is in the giving,
Truly it is worth
More than all the money
Stored upon the earth.
For every gift is priceless
No matter what its measure
And your true and loving Friendship
Is one I'll always treasure.

LYNN NEW ©

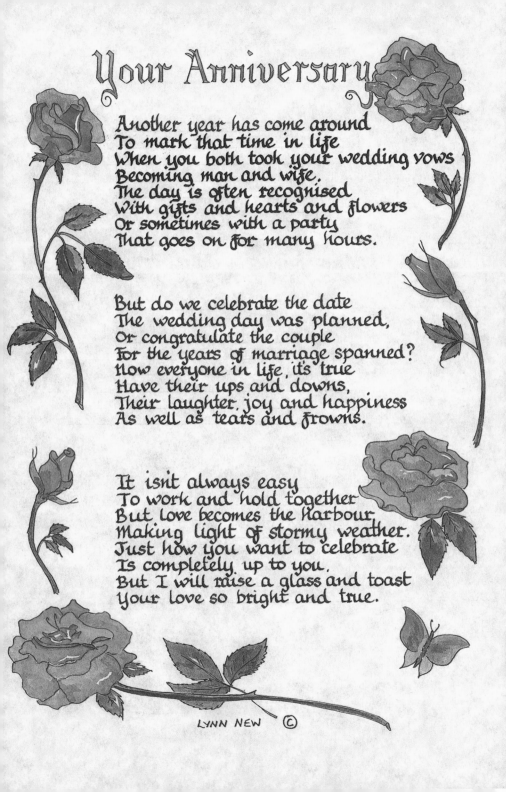

Your Anniversary

Another year has come around
To mark that time in life
When you both took your wedding vows
Becoming man and wife.
The day is often recognised
With gifts and hearts and flowers
Or sometimes with a party
That goes on for many hours.

But do we celebrate the date
The wedding day was planned,
Or congratulate the couple
For the years of marriage spanned?
Now everyone in life, it's true
Have their ups and downs,
Their laughter, joy and happiness
As well as tears and frowns.

It isn't always easy
To work and hold together
But love becomes the harbour,
Making light of stormy weather.
Just how you want to celebrate
Is completely up to you,
But I will raise a glass and toast
Your love so bright and true.

LYNN NEW ©

Comfort

And I shall be with you through the night,
Throughout your day and endless fight;
And I shall hold your hand and stay
To see you to life's brighter day.
And I shall watch beside your bed
And hold your hand and stroke your head,
Then you shall so much lighter feel
Knowing I am with you...

Our Grandson.

From reading books and playing ball
We've watched you since you were so small.
From babe in arms, to growing boy
We've shared your tears and laughing joy.

Dear grandson, how we care for you,
And always want to share with you
The times in life when you're on top,
Or give a hug when spirits drop.

So when your parents need some space,
There will be a welcome at our place;
Grandparents have their uses too,
There'll always be some room for you.

When memory's short and days are long,
You're in our hearts where you belong.
You've given us great times to treasure;
Grandson we love you, beyond measure.

No pain beyond, no tears, no fear.
No thought of death-for I'm still near.
No hugs I know, nor sweet caress,
But I'm still close to love and bless.
No quiet word, nor gentle touch
But don't despair - I love you much.
No gesture kind to show I care;
The veil's drawn, but I'm still there.
Grieve not too long - but look around
In earthly things I shall be found.
A falling leaf, a growing tree,
In every breeze you will feel me.
I walk in life; death holds no pain.
Be reassured, we'll meet again.

Remember Me.

My Wife.

I give you my heart,
Undying love, my all.
I give you my hand
If any time you fall.
I'll share with you my life,
It shall have no end
For you became my wife
My lover and my friend.

I bring to you my joy,
My laughter and my fears,
And by your side I'll walk
Through tomorrow's years.
I'll stand by you my love
Through pain and trouble,
And hope I'll halve the worry
And make your strength as double.

I'll think of you my love
When we're apart,
And count the passing hours
By my beating heart.
I'll try my very best
To be the man for you
And show my love in all I say
And everything I do.

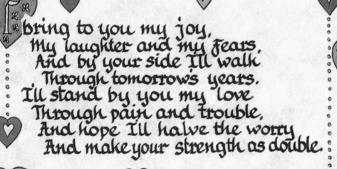

Sixtieth Celebrations

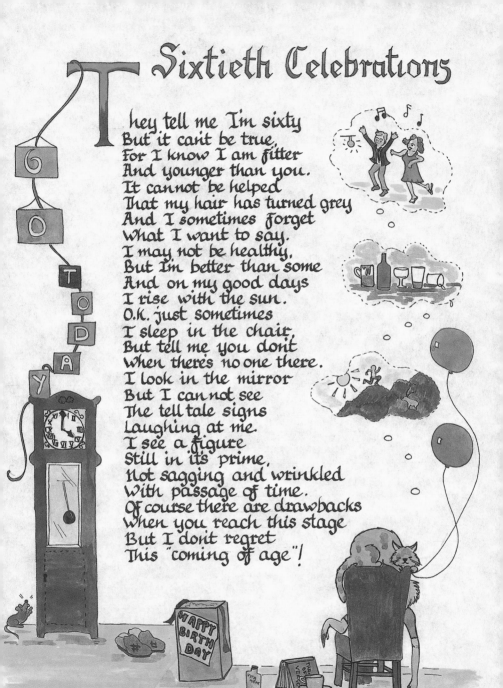

They tell me I'm sixty
But it can't be true,
For I know I am fitter
And younger than you.
It cannot be helped
That my hair has turned grey
And I sometimes forget
What I want to say.
I may not be healthy,
But I'm better than some
And on my good days
I rise with the sun.
O.K. just sometimes
I sleep in the chair,
But tell me you don't
When there's no one there.
I look in the mirror
But I can not see
The tell tale signs
Laughing at me.
I see a figure
Still in its prime,
Not sagging and wrinkled
With passage of time.
Of course there are drawbacks
When you reach this stage
But I don't regret
This "coming of age"!

LYNN NEW ©

Lovers (K)not.

Where did it go, that dream of you and I?
Written in the stars that spanned the evening sky.
Shining in full glory - a lovers fantasy;
Why did it have to fade - why did that have to be?

Who called the time on all the joy we shared,
And separated us, though we, in love were paired?
Why were the hours short and numbered days?
It seemed that once so close, now go our separate
                                                    ways.

Was my love too strong for you to bear?
Too intense by far in showing how I care?
Did we love each other too little or too well?
We will never know now - for lovers never tell.

Should we perhaps rekindle this love into a flame,
Or let the candle gutter, extinguishing the pain?
I know whatever happens - my love I cant regret
The day that you first touched me ~
            the day that first we met.

Unconditional Love.

Love must be unconditional
For truly it must be
Born of selfless giving
Spiritual and free.
Showing all encouragement
Helping smooth the way,
Catching not another's heart
And begging it to stay.

Love isn't born for smothering
For that shall snuff the flame
Extinguishing the candle light
That bears another's name.
It shouldn't be possessive
Demanding all control
But filled with sensual giving
From the spirit of the soul.

Hold not that love too tightly,
Let it rest in open hands,
For it will not take fright and fly
When it understands
There's nothing there to hurt it,
To crush its fragile wings;
For when it isn't threatened
The bird of loving sings.

Parents' Love.

Parents' love is many things,
The comfort, strength and clip of wings.
The saying no, the telling why.
The warmth untold, to touch the sky.
It is the eyes that see it all,
The ears that hear the every call.
The arms that hold, comfort to bring.
The voice to scold, or joyful sing.
It is the hand that wipes the tears
Of a child growing through the years.
A mother, father, both are one
To a daughter, or a son,
For as a pair, both play their parts,
For surely, both have loving hearts.

LYNN NEW ©

New Baby Born

Precious little child
Welcome to our world
With your skin of satin
And tiny fists uncurled.
Welcome to your parents
Whose loving arms will hold
You close in their protection
More priceless now than gold.
Welcome to the daybreak
And the birds that sing;
May you be blessed with laughter
And all that love can bring.
Welcome to the raindrops
And the warmth of sun
Knowing that life's journey
Has only just begun.

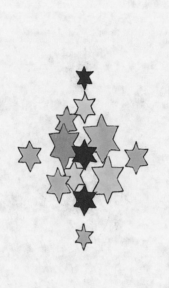

Orion's Watch

Fast falls the year, but thereby climbs Orion,
Upon the shoulders of the sky, deep velvet.
Like diamonds standing, placed by some
                   great hand
And year by year, all knowing, there they stand.
Herald the night...the autumn cold but
                   brilliant;
You can, by shape, point stars in recognition.
Great giant of the skies you silent turn
And navigators of the sea from you shall learn.
Fellow of great myth what stories do you hide?
True lovers watching as you span their gaze.
The nocturn feed of owls emerging
And gathered storm to cover you with
                   clouds converging.
Fettered fellow in the skies of brilliant autumn,
Your shoulders strong with radiance of light.
Your belt and scabbard centre you; now
                   hear my plea,
Oh silent giant of the skies...
                watch over me!

LYNN NEW ©

Your New Home.

Packets and boxes and things to unpack,
Shelves to assemble, crocks there to stack.
Curtains for hanging and carpets to lay,
Surely will take more than a day.

Cupboards for cleaning and windows to shine,
Plenty to wash, if the day remains fine.
Rummaging boxes and tea chests for treasure,
Finding the teapot will prove you are clever!

Chipping the woodwork with corners of tables,
Tripping over the doormat and telephone
cables.
Trying to smile as chaos descends,
Knowing success, on your temper depends.

But when the night falls and the curtains
you pull,
I know you'll look round with hearts that
are full.
For though you are weary as you lock the
door
You'll know that your new home is worth
working for.

LYNN NEW ©

The Rose.

Visualize this Rose I give you...
    ... I give you with Love!

Cherish the stem from which grows the Flower,
for it carries the Life force from the source
of our Father to the likeness of the child.

Cherish the thorns which grow upon the stem,
from which comes the pain and the healing
and the learning.

Rejoice for the leaves for they reach out in
welcome to Gods given rain and give shelter
and succour.

Bless the tight leaves around the bud for
they protect the sensitive and open only
when God wills the rose to show its strength
and beauty.

Cherish and rejoice, bless and behold the rose
in all its glory, each petal relates to each
chapter of life made up of dreams and
aspirations. Gods Love is the whole, each petal
part of that Love.

Breathe deeply the perfume of this rose for
it will fill the head and lungs of the many
who pass by.

Be proud of the centre of the bloom for it
shall attract the bee who shall propagate love.

I give you this rose, bless it well, nurture it
and hold it to you that it may bring you
comfort and courage for the future and perfume
your world. In giving you this rose....

    God gives you His Love.